MW00890880

SUMMARY

of

THANK YOU FOR BEING LATE

An Optimist's Guide to Thriving in the Age of Accelerations

by Thomas L. Friedman

A FastReads Book Summary with Key Takeaways & Analysis

TABLE OF CONTENTS

EXECUTIVE SUMMARY

If you're living through the 21st century but feeling like the pace of life has picked up beyond what you can handle, *Thank You for Being Late* will help you understand why. Renowned journalist Thomas L. Friedman has returned to what he does best in this fascinating field guide to modern life, though many of the conclusions he comes to might leave you feeling anything but optimistic.

People around the world can sense that things are changing fast, but it's difficult to put a finger on why. Friedman does the difficult work for you by looking through a half century of worldwide technological and geopolitical innovation in order to highlight the ways that things have changed beyond recognition- even in the last 10 years.

By explaining the exponential powers of Moore's Law for technology, the 'States of Destruction' that countries are descending into post-post-Cold War, and the devastation that environmental degradation and booming populations has caused to the natural world, Friedman points the finger at where things derailed in the modern world—and what we can do to get back on track.

By writing his book in the same format he writes his New York Times columns, Friedman sets up the problem and explains the intricacies of it through numerous interviews and personal examples for deeper understanding. Finally, he turns back to the unexpected successes of his hometown in Minnesota as an example of a way forward in building grass-root communities that can withstand the pressures of a rapidly changing world.

If you've found yourself thinking back to a time without cellphones or wondering when the robots will come for your job, *Thank You for Being Late* is a timely book for you to read. This work of contemporary history will leave you more knowledgeable about the direction the world is going and will arm you with the tools needed to start to change that trajectory when necessary.

All it takes is taking the time to slow down.

PART 1: REFLECTING

1. Thank You for Being Late

"Nothing in life is to be feared, it is only to be understood. Now is the time to understand more, so that we may fear less." Marie Curie

Friedman begins this book by writing why he went into journalism (his love of breaking down complex subjects to make them understandable). He feels that his work is more relevant now than ever, as many people feel frightened by the changes happening in the modern world—including accelerations in technology, climate change and globalization. Because of these enormous changes happening so fast, big updates need to happen in societies, workplaces and the general geopolitical situation around the world.

In a world where we've all gone from zero to sixty in about five seconds, Friedman wants to challenge us to slow down enough to pause and reflect in order to increase the odds we can understand the world around us. Friedman had this revelation in 2015 when a breakfast date showed up late and he realized he actually appreciated the time to himself to sit, think, and eavesdrop.

A similar experience of slowing down became the inspiration for this entire book. Parking his car in 2014, Friedman was stopped by a parking attendant who recognized him from his column in the New York Times. The attendant asked Friedman to look at his personal blog, which he grudgingly did. To his surprise, it was about the political situation in Ethiopia, the country the man was from. Suddenly in the age of accelerations, parking attendants were now his competition for column writing!

The two started a relationship and Friedman taught the attendant about better column writing while the attendant relayed his life story. Friedman taught him that column writing is an act of chemistry, trying to combine words together that will either create heat or light for the reader and must include the writer's own values, priorities and aspirations.

In his views, everything is interconnected. You can't understand the geopolitical tensions around the world without looking at the damage of global warming or joblessness caused by automation. In order to understand the changes, you have to look at the inner workings of the machine itself.

Key Takeaways

• Sometimes the only way to notice important things around you is to take the time to slow down.

PART II: ACCELERATING

2. What the Hell Happened in 2007

"It is the core argument of this book that these simultaneous accelerations in the Market, Mother Nature, and Moore's law together constitute the "age of accelerations," in which we now find ourselves." – Thomas L. Friedman

Friedman believes that many of the big changes we are experiencing in the world today all started in 2007, including explosions in storage capacity for computers, the start of Facebook and Twitter and the beginning of 'big data.' Most notably, 2007 was the year that the iPhone came out. Enormous changes in technology all took place within a short time frame, creating endless new ways for people to connect and collaborate with each other.

The reason behind much of this rapid change and innovation can be attributed to George Moore, who founded Moore's Law in 1965. The law states that the speed and power of microchips will double roughly every two years for just a little more money. This level of exponential growth has held true for five decades and shows no sign of slowing down.

It's easy to underestimate the exponential powers of doubling numbers, but try doubling grains of rice on each square of a chessboard, and by the time you make it to the last few squares you'll have over eighteen quintillion grains of rice. In the same way, the exponential growth of technology and innovation is starting to reach the second half of that chessboard. And this is starting to become a big problem.

It used to take centuries for technological advances to change the world, but today it takes just a few years (look at the iPhone). However, the rate that people can ADJUST to new technology hasn't grown exponentially. In most cases, people can't keep up with the changes and it leads to angst and disassociation, not to mention danger when society can't create rules to govern the technology fast enough.

Key Takeaways

• Major changes throughout different sectors of technology combined in 2007 and possibly changed the world forever.

3: Moore's Law

Understanding exponential growth is hard, but if cars were improving at the same rate of microchips, a Volkswagen Beetle today would be able to go three hundred thousand miles an hour, get two million miles per gallon of gas, and would cost just four cents. Clearly, something unique is happening with computers and microchips.

The reasons microchips keep improving is that engineers keep finding entirely new ways to make them—essentially reinventing them every 24 months. Though people keep predicting the death of Moore's Law and the plateauing of technological advancement, it simply hasn't happened yet.

Not only is technology getting more powerful, it is also changing the ways that traditional jobs are managed—meaning that cars can tell us when they need an oil change and automatic milking machines know to take care of cows only when needed. Even more impressive, sensors on cows can tell exactly when a cow is in heat, allowing the farmer to inseminate her at the exact right time, taking the guesswork out of farming. Even billboards are getting smart, meaning they can track cars that drive by and see what stores they actually start shopping at.

With technological advances has come more collaboration within innovation, meaning that open-source software is growing in popularity. Perhaps most significant, the invention of the 'cloud' as a way to wirelessly store data on networks is completely changing the potential for programs like Netflix and Microsoft Office to allow people to connect to their resources where ever they are. In fact, Friedman believes that the cloud is so transformative for life today that he prefers to call it the 'Supernova.'

Key Takeaways

• Exponential growth models are not to be underestimated—especially when you're living in one.

4: The Supernova

A human turning point took place in 2011 when a supercomputer named Watson managed to beat the world's top trivia players in Jeopardy. The age of computers being more competent than humans has officially begun. Watson ran off the power of the cloud, and this meant it had the combined power of hundreds and hundreds of computers, all in one frame.

As technology has improved, 'complexity has become free,' meaning that intricate problems like getting a taxi or finding a house in Australia to stay in are all changed through easy access technology like Uber and AirBnB. The transition from an industrial age to an information age is certainly revealing growing pains, but systems thinking is making it easier than ever to perform complicated tasks as simply as possible. There's never been a better time in history to be a maker, inventor, or innovator.

Many people get worried when they hear about computers like Watson because they assume they will take jobs away from them someday. That's not true, in IBM's (and Friedman's) opinion. Instead, they foresee supercomputers digesting enormous amounts of new research and data in specialized fields like the medical field and then aiding doctors in the decision process, while the doctor performs the human interaction side.

Computers will never replace humans, but they can help humans to do their jobs better. In fact, technology like AirBnB helps humans connect with each other better because it fosters relationships between people from around the globe.

Key Takeaways

• The rise of the supernova is causing more people to become empowered and connected with each other.

• Rather than stifling human potential, the age of computers is simply tapping into it.

5: The Market

The connections that technology is creating between people all around the world can be called "flows", and they are as useful for progress in the modern world as rivers used to be for ancient civilizations. In fact, people are so dependent on cell phones now that over a third of people surveyed claimed they would give up sex for a year to keep their phone. This dependence will only get stronger as more people are connected to machines and machines connect more to each other.

'The Big Shift' in our world today is moving away from stocks being a main form of value for a country to flows being that value. Now, countries are powerful based on how connected they are within themselves and to the rest of the world. Best of all, anyone can connect into this flow so long as they have a rudimentary internet device like a smartphone or tablet. Rural schools in developing countries can now use the resources of internet courses in Khan Academy to teach their students, which has enormous power to level the playing ground between the world's 'haves' and 'have nots.' Even Facebook has been forging millions of connections between people in nations that have been at war for decades, like Israel and Palestine.

Like it or not, the increase of technology is turning connections with each other into one of the most valuable assets in the world.

Key Takeaways

• Jobs and net value is changing around the world, and the future of success will depend on harnessing flows.

6: Mother Nature

As the years go on it's becoming increasingly clear that the age of acceleration is coming at a high cost, specifically to the natural world. Temperatures have been soaring around the planet and each passing year becomes the hottest on record. The real-world consequences of climate change are starting to be felt, in many cases decades earlier than scientists had predicted. People everywhere can tell something is different with the world, but the data between points is often too disconnected to see the larger picture. However, the full story is beginning to come together in extremely alarming clarity.

For all of human history, we have been living in the Holocene period—a time when the climate was habitable for humans. Due to global warming, the temperature and weather extremes that the planet is facing now are so beyond what is typical for the Holocene period that they have launched us into an era of living like no other time that humans have been on the planet.

These dramatic changes are due to the Great Acceleration, or the stress that humans have put on the planet as populations have surged along with the average standard of living. Planetary limits are increasingly approached and passed, getting the world closer to a precarious tipping point that might destroy every system we have come to depend on.

Key Takeaways

• Reaping the rewards of technological progress without keeping an eye open to unintended consequences is a recipe for climate disaster.

PART III: INNOVATING

7. Just Too Damned Fast

The increase rate of our lives due to technology is certainly coming at a cost, and the general population is starting to feel the pain. Friedman feels these changes personally, as his career as a journalist is almost unrecognizable now from his early days of typewriters and international fax machines. Today, he often has people reading and commenting on his international news stories before the story has even broken in the US.

The intense rate that careers are changing to keep up with technology is making an entire class of workers obsolete unless they can be lifelong learners.

Key Takeaways

• Jobs are changing beyond recognition, and the modern worker needs to stay on top of these changes.

8: Turning AI into IA

"You can be a lifelong employee if you are ready to be a lifelong learner."- Thomas L. Friedman

Despite some lingering fear, Friedman remains convinced that robots won't take every job. That doesn't mean the economy hasn't been forever changed since the easy-going 90s when it was simple to make enough money to take your kids to Disneyworld every year. College graduates don't have to simply find a job; in many cases, they actually have to invent it.

Because of this, it's becoming harder than ever to stay middle class, or even to stay relevant within the job you went to college for. No longer is it enough to be local to get a job, now you have to compete against hundreds of people around the world who can do the exact same job as you—and who can do it remotely.

However, technology isn't always bad news for competition. Adding ATMs to banks actually made it more profitable to open more branches, which worked to increase the amount of bank tellers that were hired. Bank tellers might do more human related work and fewer menial jobs now, but many more are employed than ever before—all thanks to technology. For this reason, jobs aren't going away, but the kinds of jobs that are available are going to change dramatically. In order to be a lifelong employee, it's now essentially to be able to tap into the power of the information flow and to be a lifelong learner.

The cashier jobs at McDonalds are probably going away, but the systems management and human relationship side of these jobs is never going to change, so that is the side the prospective employees need to tap into.

Key Takeaways

• Robots won't take every job, but they are guaranteed to transform the job market almost beyond recognition.

9: Control vs. Kaos

We are living in the post-post-Cold War world right now, which can be described (according to Friedman) as the world bordering on Order and Disorder. The role of America as a political power in the world has slowly been shifting as the rest of the world begins to capitalize on the economy of flows. The shifting role of the market, the natural world and Moore's Law are forever changing the way that America and other developed nations fit into the global puzzle.

Increasing terrorist attacks like 9/11 are compromising the sense of security and order in the world that has long taken it for granted. Now, a few radicalized people have the power to cause great harm to thousands, and with nuclear weapons, possibly everyone.

It used to be okay for developing countries to be 'average', but in a world of spiking populations and climate change, average is no longer good enough. This makes it simple for nations to flip into the 'World of Disorder' and political chaos, just like Egypt during the Arab Spring and today in Syria.

Much of the unrest in these countries is made worse through intense weather disasters, including decades-long droughts throughout much of Africa and the Middle East. As people continue to be displaced because the climate makes it impossible to survive on their farms, regions like Europe are facing a massive influx of refugees and are being stretched thin to care for them.

Though the rise of social networks is an incredible way to instigate change (like Facebook during the Arab Spring) it comes with challenges as well. Social media tends to lead to group polarizing (selecting communities based on people that think like you) and can create 'echo chambers' of assent. In the long run, though social media mobilized the efforts of Egyptian youth and allowed them to connect with each other, it failed to create a platform for them to come together and create the stable governance they were seeking.

The flow also complicates international dealings with terrorist groups, as ISIS largely exists online and doesn't have a centralized location in the physical world that can be taken out. Killing off some leaders only causes others to rise up and fill the vacuum.

In a post-post-Cold War world, long term changes need to start small. For the world's poorest people, owning a chicken can make an enormous difference in their livelihood, and creating international programs to meet these basic agrarian needs can make a huge difference.

Key Takeaways

• An increasingly interconnected world creates incredible opportunities for international growth or destruction, depending on how the flows of information are harnessed.

10: Mother Nature as Political Mentor

"It is not the strongest species that survives but the most adaptable."

In an age of uncertainty, Americans have been turning towards people outside the system, especially in politics. During the 2016 primaries, Bernie Sanders promised to "take down the man" while Donald Trump vowed to "be the man." It's little wonder more moderate candidates that represented the status quo were rejected in favor of these antiestablishment politicians.

Looking to nature is a smart way to understand how to survive periods of intense change. On average, 99% of what Mother Nature attempts fails, but through the process of constant innovation she stumbles on some incredible solutions that we would be wise to copy.

According to Friedman, Mother Nature has five killer apps that have allowed her to thrive for three billion years, and we would be smart to emulate her example.

1. Being adaptive when confronted with strangers or the need to change.

2. Embracing diversity

3. Creating cultures of ownership

4. Striking a proper balance between levels of government

5. Forming political parties based on entrepreneur mindsets looking for innovation

In order for America to survive the Age of Accelerations, it will be essential to copy the example of Mother Nature in every way that we can.

Key Takeaways

• When looking to a model of how to manage the modern world, no example has better stood the test of time than Mother Nature herself.

11: Is God in Cyberspace?

"There has never ever been a time when the human being was capable of doing something and yet, eventually, that something did not happen. That means one of three things: 1) the human psyche is going to change fundamentally (good luck with that!); 2) the worldwide social contract changes so that the "angry men" can no longer be "empowered" (good luck with that too!); or 3) boom!" - Garrett Andrews

Friedman was asked about the role of God in the internet during one of his lectures, and the question stuck with him for years. If you look at the amount of crime, pornography and scam artists on the web, it's obvious to him that God ISN'T present. Yet, Friedman believes, God wants to be there. The internet can unify mankind and make us free, but this freedom without the presence of God is a terrifying thought.

Since the dropping of the nuclear bombs in 1945, humanity has been playing God to itself. Now scientists have the power to make mosquito species extinct if they want to. Learning to manage the power of a world so free is startling, but it's a challenge that we all need to take on. The time has come for communities to rise up and instill the values into young people that are needed for them to act as responsible global citizens in an increasingly uncertain world.

Key Takeaways

• In many ways, humans have taken on the power of God in the modern world.

12: Always Looking for Minnesota

In the Age of Accelerations, we are in the midst of a hurricane. The only moments of peace can be found by keeping ourselves in the eye and allowing the storm to rage around us. For Friedman, the eye of the hurricane can be found through the fostering of healthy communities. Communities create feedback loops and accountability to prevent people from feeling isolated or ignored, and can help to create the behaviors on a small scale that the world needs overall. For this reason, the world often looks better from the bottom up than the top down.

Friedman found this community in his hometown of St. Louis Park in Minnesota, a place that accepted the outsider (a growing Jewish population) and was filled with coaches and teachers that worked as role models for the youth growing up. Friedman was exposed to businessmen while caddying on golf courses and learned how that world worked, so even in the midst of mild anti-Semitism he felt empowered.

Positive relationships with African-Americans moved faster there than the rest of the nation as well, as "Minnesota nice" sensitivities caused people to be more willing to open their homes to outsiders. Friedman also credits high quality public spaces for fostering a greater sense of community because people had places outside of their homes and work to meet and interact with each other.

Friedman attributes much of the success of his hometown to a strong middle class that was easy for outsiders to enter into. This has left him with a lifelong bias towards optimism that things can work out when broadly shared ideals are acted on by society.

Key Takeaways

• Reiterate important information to avoid accidental forgetting, and gradually introduce new information to coerce your audience to forget old methods.

• Map out potential trends and create content that addresses these trends to become a part of your audience's future.

• Anticipate disruptions to build new content, memories and cues.

13. You Can Go Home Again (and You Should!)

After another encounter with a parking attendant, Friedman was both surprised and pleased to learn that the Somali-born man felt that Minnesota was a welcoming home to him too.

The high quality political leaders in Minnesota came into power during a critical time in the state's history and transformed the culture of community for years after. These politicians were similar in their willingness to compromise with each other in order to get things done for the common good, and this desire to produce results for the good of all also extended into the business/private sectors. In fact, when an investment on solar panels for the city didn't work out, those that voted against the measure issued condolences to the community rather than rubbing in that they were right to begin with.

This culture has made Minnesota a smart place to settle for families of all cultures for decades, and it has set a standard that the rest of the US needs to quickly catch up with in order to thrive through the age of accelerations. By extension, long term change needs to happen at the community level, which is why people across America and around the world need to go back to their roots, build community gardens and vote in local elections. Small changes like this help to build a thriving sense of community that makes chaos, uncertainty and the fear of the 'other' much easier to cope with.

In order for this to work, cultural uniqueness needs to be celebrated, especially in the case of immigrants. The cultural melting pot doesn't need to make everyone the same. However, there needs to be some consistency or bedrock values between people within a community (things like women's rights and other shared values), otherwise the first hint of tension will cause a community to fracture apart.

Key Takeaways

• Before looking at ways to transform the future, it's important to study what worked in the past.

PART IV: ANCHORING

14: From Minnesota to the World and Back

Though the ideas for this book were rolling around in Friedman's head for several years, it took chance encounters with a parking attendant to get him to make it happen.

As the world continues to change and the types of jobs available to the average person continue to evolve beyond recognition, the world that exists is one where you need a plan to succeed. The world is moving fast, and little movements in the wrong direction can be enough to get us all wildly off track.

The world of the future is one dependent on both STEM sciences and chicken coops. It's a world of almost immeasurable connections, yet the vast majority of Americans still feel isolated and alone. Transitions are always difficult to maneuver. After all, the most dangerous time to be on the streets of New York City was when cars were coming on the scene but horses and buggies were not yet phased out. The 21st century will be full of challenges, but with a unification of the global human spirit, no challenge should be insurmountable.

Key Takeaways

• The stakes might be higher, but the challenges aren't new. With resolve, unification and a strong plan in place the world can master the changes of the Age of Accelerations.

EDITORIAL REVIEW

Thank You for Being Late by Thomas Friedman is a fascinating summary of the past five decades of human history, which has been one of the most significant eras for the shaping what the world will look like in the future. Though Friedman claims to be an optimist throughout his writing, many of the conclusions that he comes to are scarily sinister and leave the reader with the sense that the world is about to get a lot more terrifying before things get better.

Friedman is at his best when he writes about the history of modern technology and the global geopolitical situation, and at his worst when trying to tie in pithy experiences of his own life into his writing. Frankly, the subject matter Friedman is covering is fascinating enough without him so frequently needing to depend on the tales of inspiration parking lot attendants as a crutch.

Another concern is the ironic truth that Friedman's book about the rapidly changing pace of today's world is already somewhat out of date just a few weeks after being released. For example, he spends a decent amount of time explaining the implications of the 2016 US presidential election, but it's obvious that everything is written from the lens that now President-elect Donald Trump was a passing fad who would lose the race. In the wake of the shocking election results, many of Friedman's conclusions about the future state of American politics will need to be reconsidered.

That being said, *Thank You for Being Late* is worth the read and will offer valuable insight to the reader as to why the world looks so different today than it did even in 2007. Though much of this book will leave the reader with a sense of dread about the current state of the world, Friedman offers enough positive insights to produce some hope for the future.

In light of this acceleration, one can only wonder what new world changes Friedman's ten year update of this book will touch on.

END

If you enjoyed this summary, please leave an honest review on Amazon.com! It'd mean a lot to us!

Here are some other available titles from FastReads we think you'll enjoy:

Summary of The Hard Thing About Hard Things
by Ben Horowitz

Summary of The Third Wave
by Steve Case

Summary of How to Fail at Almost Everything
by Scott Adams

Summary of The Inevitable
by Kevin Kelly

Summary of The Checklist Manifesto
by Atul Gawande

Made in the USA
Middletown, DE
03 May 2017